Christmas Poems

Fiona Waters is one of the most prolific and very best anthologists in the children's book world. Her work includes *Glitter When You Jump, Love, Don't Panic: 100 Poems to Save Your Life, Wizard Poems* and *Best Friends*. Her unparalleled knowledge of poetry and children's books has come about, in part, through Fiona's previous incarnations as a bookseller, publisher, reviewer, author and current position as Editorial Director of Troubadour, the highly successful school book-fair company.

Fiona lives in Dorset surrounded by thousands of books and some very discerning cats.

Christmas Poems

Chosen by Fiona Waters

Illustrated by Lara Jones

MACMILLAN CHILDREN'S BOOKS

For Ruby, with much love from her Great-Aunt Fiona

First published 2006 by Macmillan Children's Books
a division of Macmillan Publishers Limited
20 New Wharf Road, London N1 9RR
Basingstoke and Oxford
www.panmacmillan.com

Associated companies throughout the world

ISBN-13: 978-0-330-44288-6
ISBN-10: 0-330-44288-0

3 5 7 9 8 6 4

A CIP catalogue record for this book is available from
the British Library.

Typeset by Perfect Bound Ltd
Printed and bound in Great Britain by CPI Mackays, Chatham ME5 8TD

Visit **www.panmacmillan.com** to read more about all our books and to buy
them. You will also find features, author interviews and news of any author
events, and you can sign up for e-newsletters so that you're always first to hear
about our new releases.

Contents

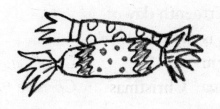

Snow

Silent raider
Earth invader

Whiteness spreader
Sunshine dreader

Edges blurrer
Sledges bearer

Winter dresser
Christmas blesser

Graham Denton

I Really Would Like to Be Mary

I really would like to be Mary –
The very best part in the play.
I could sit by the crib with my baby,
Centre stage! With nothing to say!

I wouldn't mind being an angel,
With wings, and a halo that shines.
I could stand at the back looking holy,
And memorize everyone's lines.

I wouldn't mind being a snowflake,
With a doily pinned over my hair;
Or a pageboy, with myrrh on a cushion,
And a tea-cosy turban to wear.

I wouldn't mind being a robin,
With a patch of red stuck to my chest;
Or a camel wrapped up in a blanket,
With a bulge in the back of my vest.

I wouldn't mind being narrator,
Provided the words weren't too long;
Or the person who crashes the cymbals
When we come to the end of our song.

I would mind selling the programmes –
No, any old part would suit me . . .
So can anyone answer my question:
Why is it I'm ALWAYS a tree?

Clare Bevan

Musical Chairs

Mum tells me we can play musical chairs
At my Christmas party next week.
But none of our chairs knows any good
  tunes.
They just groan a little or squeak.

Barry Buckingham

What Is It?

Is that a meteor flashing
through the night on Christmas Eve?
Or is a rocket shooting by,
a wonder to perceive?
Or could a falling satellite
be flaring round its edge?
No, no!
That's modern Santa
in his supersonic,
air-conditioned,
friction-heated,
CD-playing,
rocket-motored,
turbo-boosted sledge.

Barry Buckingham

A Reindeer Rap

We're a groovy team,
We're a hot hoof band
With our jingle bells
From a magic land.
When we pull that sleigh,
When we go, man, go,
When we bring F.C.
With his Ho! Ho! Ho!
When we get on down
To your sleepy street,
When we rock your roof
To a hip-hop beat,
When we stomp away
Through the starry sky
You can make a wish
As we boogie by.
You can shake your hands,
You can stamp your toe,
You can strut your stuff
In the cool Yule snow,

You can shout and cheer,
Set the whole world clapping –
We're the Reindeer Band
And we're Christmas Rapping!

Clare Bevan

The Christmas Feeling

Why can't we have the Christmas
Feeling all through the year?
The days before Christmas
When we sing of good cheer.

When anticipation
Seems to float in the air,
Strangers greet each other
And really seem to care.

When people look happy
And the smiles stay in place,
Brightening up their eyes,
Bringing a glow to each face.

In the street bands play carols,
And the passers-by sing.
It could last much longer,
Don't let the New Year in.

Pat Gadsby

Sans Day Carol

Now the holly bears a berry as white as the
   milk,
And Mary bore Jesus, who was wrapped up
   in silk:

*And Mary bore Jesus Christ our Saviour for
   to be,*
*And the first tree in the greenwood, it was
   the holly, holly, holly,*
*And the first tree in the greenwood, it was
   the holly.*

Now the holly bears a berry as green as the
   grass,
And Mary bore Jesus, who died on the cross:

*And Mary bore Jesus Christ our Saviour for
   to be,*
*And the first tree in the greenwood, it was
   the holly, holly, holly,*
*And the first tree in the greenwood, it was
   the holly.*

Now the holly bears a berry as blood is it
   red,
Then trust we our Saviour, who rose from
   the dead:

And Mary bore Jesus Christ our Saviour
   for to be,
And the first tree in the greenwood, it was
   the holly, holly, holly,
And the first tree in the greenwood, it was
   the holly.

Traditional Cornish

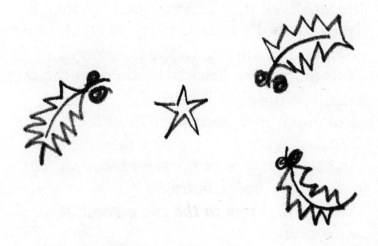

Decoration Day

Dust dances in December's dreary light
up in the attic where the mice, at night,
are heard to chase, claws scrabbling on
   the floor
and scratching at the chest whose stiff-
   joint jaw
yawns with a creak as rusty locks snap
   back
and children lift its lid to seek a sack
of rough, red cloth that bulges, clinks
   within,
and smells of pine leaves – sharper than a
   pin
on fumbling fingers. In the darkening
   room
a thrill of tinsel spills into the gloom.

Gina Douthwaite

I Thought I Saw...

I thought I saw a little Christmas pudding
  on a wall.
But no!
It was a fluffed-up robin sitting there,
  that's all.

I thought I saw a Christmas cracker
  walking on a lead.
But no!
It was a dachshund in a coat of tartan
  tweed.

I thought I saw a Christmas parcel
    swinging through the trees.
But no!
It was a squirrel wearing fancy dungarees.

I thought I saw a Christmas tree beside
    the garden shed.
But no!
It was a monster thistle growing there
    instead.

I thought I heard some carol singers
    singing a refrain.
But no!
It was a house alarm from somewhere
    down the lane.

I thought I spotted starlit Santa zooming
    through the sky.
But no!
It was a helicopter swiftly passing by.

I thought I saw a super snowman by the
 garden gate.
But no!
It was the milkman frozen solid, stiff and
 straight.

I thought I saw it snowing after dinner,
 Christmas Day.
It was!
But I was too full up to rush outside and
 play.

Barry Buckingham

Christmas Music

Ten notes of music,
like snowflakes, drift and climb.

One rests on the wing of an angel
and that leaves nine.

Nine notes of music
sparkle bright and late.

One becomes the Christmas Star
and that leaves eight.

Eight notes of music,
carols sung in Devon.

One glides away on a moonbeam
and that leaves seven.

Seven notes of music,
curved as holly sticks.

One makes a shelter for a robin
and that leaves six.

Six notes of music
soar and twirl and dive.

One nestles in Mother Earth's arms
and that leaves five.

Five notes of music
chant old solstice lore.

One gets lost in the mountains
and that leaves four.

Four notes of music,
crystals on a tree.

One is melted by winter sun
and that leaves three.

Three notes of music:
crimson, silver, blue.

One rests on top of a fir tree
and that leaves two.

Two notes of music
children call in fun.

One whistled off by a snowman
and that leaves one.

One note of music
through all space and time

links us in love
at winter's festival . . .
      Christmas song and rhyme.

Joan Poulson

Favourite Christmas Tree

We bought a tree with roots
that we could plant outside after
   Christmas
and, in its green pine branches, found
a tiny domed nest.
'It must have been built in spring
by a wren,' Mum said.

The feathers were still soft.
Little twigs and bits of moss
were twined, woven so beautifully
I didn't want to cover it with lights or
   take it inside,
away from other growing things.

'Let's plant it now!' I cried.
'Here, in our garden, and every year
we'll cover it with nuts and fat . . .
On Christmas Eve we'll put one star on
   top
so all the birds will come to feast,
welcoming Christmas Day.

And at midnight, when animals can speak,
the birds will say:
"Share with us, we have enough for all."

That night, small rustlings woke me, very
    late
and through the window I saw white
    birds
like snowflakes, fluttering everywhere,
and Earth chuckled,
warm beneath her coverlet of animals . . .

The tree shone diamond-bright, lit with
    icicles,
and jay and jackdaw, robin, song-thrush,
    finch,
birds of every sort pulled at fresh sweet
    nuts
and seeds we'd hung. And some they
    dropped
to make a ground-spread feast.

Then a wren bobbed from the branches –
soft brown feathers aglow, touched with
  gold
and on the tree three stars appeared
lighting the night,
lighting everything I could see

and everything, everywhere . . .
shining
in me.

Joan Poulson

The Christmas Olympics

Day 1. Card-opening ceremony.

Day 2. Queue jumping.

Day 3. Supermarket sprint.

Day 4. Synchronized stocking filling.

Day 5. Reindeer marathon.

Day 6. Turkey lifting.
Dessert triathlon (pudding, mince
pie, trifle).

Day 7. Recycling.

Sue Cowling

Wanted:
A Real High-Flyer!

We are seeking to recruit an enthusiastic and energetic individual to help us maintain a highly successful home-delivery service.

The ideal candidate will join a small but committed and dynamic team based at our North Pole offices.

The job will involve some unsociable hours and inclement weather, with various duties, including the lifting and transporting of existing stockings.

Applicants must be willing to travel long distances and be capable of meeting tight installation deadlines.

You will also possess excellent communication skills
(with a good understanding of the command *"Whooooaaa, boy"*), a clean sleigh-pulling licence and a perfect sense of direction.

A background in "haulage" work, a liking for snow and previous experience of icy rooftops are a distinct advantage.

This is a seasonal opportunity with an excellent holiday package.

It is a temporary position only, though is expected to lead to a more "stable" position due to the ongoing popularity of Christmas.

Starting salary dependent on age and fondness for raw carrots.

Please provide two glowing references (and, preferably, proof of glowing nose) with your application.

If you want to help us deliver quality goods to homes all over the world then please apply now to:

Santa Claus,
c/o The "Steering Committee"
Presents Unlimited
Christmas Corner
North Pole

NB Interviews to be held on December 24th with view to immediate start.

Graham Denton

What the Youngest Angel Said

Oh, how could I forget that amazing
   night?
There were hundreds of us. It was my first
   flight.

We sang to some shepherds just before
   dawn,
Then flew on to the place where the child
   was born.

I was so excited about what we'd find
That I very nearly got left behind.

It wasn't a palace or a great hall,
But a barn or a stable with a cattle stall.

I saw the mother, Mary (her face was lit
   with joy),
And an ox and a donkey, and the little
   baby boy.

Joseph stood by, he nodded and smiled;
And there were some kings who knelt to
the child.

He was swaddled in hay like a bird in its
nest.
Oh, the baby was nice. But I liked the
donkey best.

Gerard Benson

Merry Chrismix

Weather crackling.
Sleigh bells humming.
Vicar twinkling.
Robins praying.
Frost photographing.
Holly heating.
Slippers glowing.
Logs glinting.
Candles ringing.
Tinsel playing.
Angels snoring.
Santa baa-ing.
Music unwrapping.
Computers smiling.
Dogs dancing.
Stockings watching.
Presents visiting.
Dad crumbling.
Mince pies dangling.
Grandma barking.
Carol singers shining.
Mulled wine yawning.

Stars warming.
Shepherds hanging.
Sheep flying.
Biscuits raining.
Turkey singing.
Pudding hopping.
House burning.
Children cooking.

*(Unscramble this list of Christmas activities
to make your own version.)*

John Rice

Christmas Day Haiku

First chime of midnight,
starlight falls on a dark door.
Christmas Day's light knock.

John Rice

under

under the crocus and catkin   the cherry blossom
under the cherry blossom   the heat of summer
under the heat of summer   the autumn damp
under the autumn damp   the winter chill
under the winter chill   the Christmas light
the Christmas light   the Christmas light

Fred Sedgwick

The Village

The village still
beneath the hill
dressed in white
wrapped in night

A pigeon flaps
its paper wings
church bells chime
the village sings

Home from Mass
up the stairs
the village sleeps
quite unaware

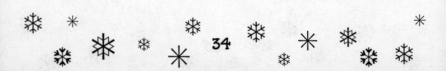

A stranger comes
but not by road
to pass around
his heavy load

More snow falls
day is dawning
the village wakes:
Christmas morning

James Carter

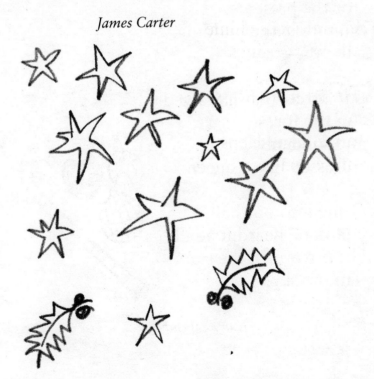

The Tree

What's the best thing
  about Christmas?
What silvery shape
  have you seen?

It wasn't the cards
  or the presents,
the carols, the pudding,
  the pie –

But a tree, that had lived
  in the forest,
and suddenly
  dressed like a queen

Came into our hall.
  No one heard it at all,
but it wore all the stars
  in the sky!

Jean Kenward

Christmas Eve Conversation

Mum! Mum!
What are the stars made of?

> Oh . . . icicles and diamonds
> All scrunched up with dew.

Mum! Mum!
Why are Christmas trees so green?

> Um . . . Christmas fairies paint them
> With emeralds stewed in spinach.

Mum! Mum!
How big are angels' wings?

> Ah . . . as big as the whole world,
> And as tiny as your fingernail.

Mum! Mum!
D'you ever tell me fibs?

Yes, my love, I do! I do!
But not when I say that I LOVE YOU.

Jennifer Curry

The Colour of Christmas

Red for Santa's scarlet hood,
Red for the holly berries in the wood,
Red for the robin's crimson breast,
Red is the colour I love the best.

Red for the wrapping paper bright,
Red for flames in the firelight,
Red for the stocking at the foot of the bed,
It's the colour of Christmas, the colour
   red.

Gervase Phinn

They Are Waiting

They are waiting
For the baby
For the baby to be born.
They are waiting in the stable
Where the cows breathe
Soft and warm.

They are waiting in the starlight
On the hills
Outside the town.
Sudden angels
Startle shepherds
Shining angels streaming down.

Flying golden
Flying silver
Pouring songs like waterfalls.
Diamond music
Telling stories
Of how God has come for all.

For the hungry
For the lonely
To fill the sad with heaven's joy.
Of how God
Is born among us
Born a helpless baby boy.

Jan Dean

We Wish You a Merry Christmas

We wish you a merry Christmas,
We wish you a merry Christmas,
We wish you a merry Christmas,
And a happy New Year.

Good tidings we bring
To you and your kin,
We wish you a merry Christmas,
And a happy New Year.

Now bring us some figgy pudding,
Now bring us some figgy pudding,
Now bring us some figgy pudding,
And bring some out here.

Chorus

For we all like figgy pudding,
For we all like figgy pudding,
For we all like figgy pudding,
So bring some out here.

Chorus

And we won't go until we've had some,
And we won't go until we've had some,
And we won't go until we've had some,
So bring some out here.

Chorus

Traditional

Haiku

avalanche of love
awakening of angels
a Baby is born

Celia Warren

One Star

Mary's son
Just begun

Straw bed
Tiny head

Shepherds keep
Sleepy sheep

Dark night
Angel light

Sent them
To Bethlehem

One star
Travelled far

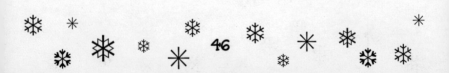

Three kings
Brought things

The light of heaven's starry skies
Shines in this small baby's eyes.

Jan Dean

Christmas Morning

On Christmas morning
we got up really early
and took the dog for a walk
across the downs

It wasn't snowing
but the hills were white with frost
and our breath froze
in the air

Judy rushed around like a mad thing
as though Christmas
meant something to her

And the sheep huddled together
looking tired
as if they'd been up all night
watching the sky
for angels

Roger Stevens

Snowflakes

Snowflakes change things
When they fall
Snowflakes hide things
From us all

Patricia P. Jones

Christmas Kisses

It's Christmas day and I'm stuck below
The dreaded bunch of mistletoe

First to attack is Auntie Rose
Who stabs my cheek with her pointy nose

I fail to avoid my Auntie Grace
Who smears her lipstick all over my face

She's not as bad as Granny Flynn
Who scratches my face with her bristly
   chin

The next kiss leaves me a nervous wreck
Uncle Pete blowing raspberries down my
  neck

And the final kiss is wet and soggy
As I'm slobbered on by Jet, our doggy.

John Coldwell

Bearing Gifts

If the babe was born in Greenland
would Eskimos have come?
Polar bears and walrus,
  seals and everyone?

Would the stable be an igloo
with snowmen from afar?
Oil
and fur
and whalebone

beneath the great
North Star?

Peter Dixon

Christmas Cat

I've built a cuddly snowcat
With whiskers made from straws –
And I'm almost sure,
I'm *almost* sure
I saw him lick his paws.

He's sitting in my garden,
He's smiling at me now,
And I'm almost sure,
I'm *almost* sure
I heard him say, "Mee-ow!"

Clare Bevan

Viscum Album

I know
They call it mistle-toe,
But it hangs
Overhead.

And so
It should be mistle-nose,
Or kissle-nose
Instead.

Ian Larmont

The First
Christmas Present

Jesus sleeps silently and soundly
Peaceful in his manger
Unaware that he has received
The first Christmas presents ever
In the history of the world

Paul Cookson

The Twelve Leftovers
of Christmas

On the twelfth day of Christmas
I found upon the floor

12 sprouts a-hiding
11 toys a-broken
10 cardboard boxes
9 lights not working
8 dented baubles
7 mince pies moulding
6 tins of biscuits
5 pairs of socks!
4 cards unposted
3 selection boxes
2 sacks of paper
And a turkey we couldn't quite eat.

Paul Cookson

On the thirteenth day of Christmas my true love phoned me up . . .

Well, I suppose I should be grateful,
    you've obviously gone
to a lot of trouble and expense –
    or maybe off your head.
Yes, I did like the birds – the small ones
    anyway were fun
if rather messy, but now the hens
    have roosted on my bed
and the rest are nested on the wardrobe.
    It's hard to sleep
with all that cooing, let alone
    the cackling of the geese,
whose eggs are everywhere,
    but mostly in a broken smelly heap
on the sofa. No, why should I mind?
    I can't get any peace
anywhere – the lounge is full
    of drummers thumping tom-toms
and sprawling lords crashed out

from manic leaping. The kitchen
is crammed with cows and milkmaids
   and smells of a million stink bombs
and enough sour milk to last a year.
   The pipers? I'd forgotten them –
they were no trouble, I paid them
   and they went. But I can't get rid
of these young ladies. They won't stop
   dancing or turn the music down
and they're always in the bathroom,
   squealing as they skid
across the flooded floor. No, I don't need a
   plumber round,
it's just the swans – where else can they
   swim? Poor things,
I think they're going mad, like me.

When I went to wash my
hands one ate the soap, another swallowed
the gold rings.
And the pear tree died. Too dry. So thanks
for nothing, love. Goodbye.

Dave Calder

Putting Away Christmas

The cards sit in a pile – a child,
dressed as a Christmas pudding,
walks along the top.

The tree lies outside –
pointing the way
for a council collection.

The fairy lights are curled up
inside their plastic box,
resting their filaments for another year.

Time to fold gold wrapping into bags,
read instructions on presents,
press my finger

on the last crumbs
of the Christmas cake
and lick the sweetness away.

Chrissie Gittins

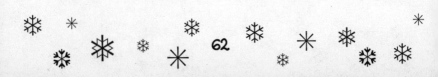

What Is Christmas?

Christmas is a lighted island
In the sea of winter darkness.

Christmas is the reindeer clatter
On the roof of the rustling house.

Christmas is the spiced kitchen
Spreading through the waiting days.

Christmas is the tongue teased
And the tummy truly tested.

Christmas is the warm hug
That wraps me in my family's love.

John Corben

Christmas Tree Needles

Long and green and sharp and thin
They give us away when we've been in
Feeling our presents under the tree
The backs of our jumpers are FORESTS

Hiawyn Oram

Will There Be Snow?

The cake's been iced
and the pudding's in the pot.
We've baked mince pies,
yes, we've made quite a lot.
Everything's ready.
There's two days to go.
But there's one last thing
I'm bursting to know:
Oh, will there be, will there be,
will there be snow?

The mistletoe's up
and the cards are strung.
The tree decorations
have all been hung.
Everything's ready.
There's two days to go.
But there's one last thing
I'm bursting to know:
Oh, will there be, will there be,
will there be snow?

There might be sleet
or there might be rain.
There might be wind
that rattles at the pane.
There might be a bright
blue sky, with sun.
But when it's Christmas
what's really fun . . .
is snow, snow, thick, thick snow,
a layer of white, I love it so!

Tony Mitton

The Christmas Mouse

A Christmas mouse
Came to our house,
Looking for crumbs
That clumsy thumbs
Had dropped on the floor.
Under the door
He quietly crept
And bits not swept
He nibbled and sniffed,
"A Christmas gift,"
Old Mousie thought,
And went and brought
His relations and friends
To share the ends
Of our Christmas feast.

Daphne Lister

The Little Drummer Boy

Come they told me, pa-rum, pum pum pum,
A newborn King to see, pa-rum, pum pum
    pum,
Our finest gifts we bring, pa-rum, pum pum
    pum,
To lay before the King, pa-rum, pum pum
    pum, rum, pum pum pum, rum, pum
    pum pum,
So to honour Him, pa-rum, pum pum pum,
When we come.

Little Baby, pa-rum, pum pum pum,
I am a poor boy too, pa-rum, pum pum
    pum,
I have no gift to bring, pa-rum, pum pum
    pum,
That's fit to give to our King, pa-rum, pum
    pum pum, rum, pum pum pum, rum,
    pum pum pum,
Shall I play for you, pa-rum, pum pum pum,
On my drum?

Mary nodded, pa-rum, pum pum pum,
The ox and lamb kept time, pa-rum, pum
    pum pum,
I played my drum for Him, pa-rum, pum
    pum pum,
I played my best for Him, pa-rum, pum
    pum pum, rum, pum pum pum, rum,
    pum pum pum,
Then He smiled at me, pa-rum, pum pum
    pum,
Me and my drum!

Harry Simeone, Henry Onorati and
Katherine K. Davis

Little Donkey

Little donkey, little donkey,
On the dusty road,
Got to keep on plodding onwards
With your precious load.
Been a long time, little donkey,
Through the winter's night.
Don't give up now, little donkey,
Bethlehem's in sight.

Ring out those bells tonight,
Bethlehem, Bethlehem.
Follow that star tonight,
Bethlehem, Bethlehem.
Little donkey, little donkey,
Had a heavy day.
Little donkey, carry Mary
Safely on her way.

Little donkey, carry Mary
Safely on her way.

Eric Boswell

Christmas Secrets

Secrets long and secrets wide,
brightly wrapped and tightly tied,

Secrets fat and secrets thin,
boxed and sealed and hidden in,

Some that rattle, some that squeak,
some that caution "Do Not Peek" . . .
Hurry, Christmas, get here first,
get here fast . . . before we *burst*.

Aileen Fisher

A Gift from the Stars

On Christmas Eve, on the first chime of
  midnight,
the Christmas King and Queen of
  Christmas
take the new moon, sharp as a blade,
and slit the thin paper sky.

They help each other wrap up the frosty
  stars
in the night's dark blue wrapping paper;
the Queen stretches out her sparkling
  hand
and grasps a passing comet to use as a gift
  tag.

The Queen of Christmas and the
  Christmas King
then take their present on a long journey:
they slide past icy meteorites,
they glide between the glassy suns,
they slink in and out of cosmic clouds,
they skim the outer edges of planets' rings

making their way through the caves and
  caverns of endless space
to this shining Earth
to this cold country
to this snowy town
to this still street
to this sleeping house
to this quiet bedroom
to this soft bed
and place their sky gift on your pillow.

John Rice

The Waiting Game

Nuts and marbles in the toe,
An orange in the heel,
A Christmas stocking in the dark
Is wonderful to feel.

Shadowy, bulging length of leg
That crackles when you clutch,
A Christmas stocking in the dark
Is marvellous to touch.

You lie back on your pillow
But that shape's still hanging there.
A Christmas stocking in the dark
Is very hard to bear,

So try to get to sleep again
And chase the hours away.
A Christmas stocking in the dark
Must wait for Christmas Day.

John Mole

Christmas Eve

I'm trying to sleep but my eyelids won't
    close
And I can't help but peep, for in front of
    my nose
Is a long woolly stocking that's red.
If I don't fall asleep Father Christmas
    won't come
And he won't eat the sandwiches made by
    my mum,
Or put toys at the end of my bed.

Michelle Magorian

Christmas Tree

Up a heavy wooded hill
A brother and sister go
As on a new adventure,
Climbing through a foot of snow.

Their faces shine; their axe is gleaming.
All morning seems to be their nurture.
They inspect the winter world
As if they were out to conquer nature.

Hand and helve now have their will.
They cut a Christmas tree from earth,
Two children shouldering home the trophy
To give the tree symbolic birth.

Then worshipping, not knowing,
With lights, and games, and gifts, they play
Lightly, in their youthful growing,
Nor climb to confront divinity.

Richard Eberhart

Questions on Christmas Eve

But *how* can his reindeer fly without wings?
Jets on their hooves? That's plain cheating!
And *how* can he climb down the chimney
   pot
  When we've got central heating?

You say it's all magic and I shouldn't ask
About Santa on Christmas Eve.
But I'm confused by the stories I've heard;
  I don't know what to believe.

I said that I'd sit up in bed all night long
To see if he really would call.
But I fell fast asleep, woke up after dawn
  As something banged in the hall.

I saw my sock crammed with apples and
　　sweets;
There were parcels piled high near the door.
Jingle bells tinkled far off in the dark;
　One snowflake shone on the floor.

Wes Magee

Thomas's First Christingle

Thomas is holding
an orange world in his hand
and trying to keep
the candle on top upright.

He touches red ribbon, raisins, nuts
               – what's it all mean?
"The next bit's magic,"
his sister, Ann, whispers.
"Wait and see!"

In a big circle
all round the pews they stand:
mums, dads, children,
grandparents packed in tight.
One by one the candles are lit
and someone . . .
switches out the church lights!

In the darkness
the Christingle circle glows,
Christ's light
shining on each single face.

Patricia Leighton

Christmas Is Coming

Christmas is coming,
  The geese are getting fat,
Please put a penny
  In the old man's hat.
If you haven't got a penny,
  A ha'penny will do;
If you haven't got a ha'penny,
  Then God bless you!

Anon.

The Rocking Carol

Little Jesus, sweetly sleep, do not stir;
We will lend a coat of fur,
   We will rock you, rock you, rock you,
   We will rock you, rock you, rock you:
See the fur to keep you warm
Snugly round your tiny form.

Mary's little baby, sleep, sweetly sleep,
Sleep in comfort, slumber deep,
   We will rock you, rock you, rock you,
   We will rock you, rock you, rock you:
We will serve you all we can,
Darling, darling little man.

Percy Dearmer

Space Poems

Chosen by
Gaby Morgan

Blast off into outer space with this brilliant collection
of poems about stars, rockets, space explorers,
planets, aliens and the moon.

Space Counting Rhyme

10 flying saucers, 10 flashing lights
9 glowing trails, 9 meteorites
8 silver spaceships trying to find
7 lost aliens left behind
6 burning comets blazing fire
5 red rockets blasting higher
4 satellites, 4 radar dishes
3 stars shooting means 3 wishes
2 bright lights – the moon and sun
1 little me to shine upon

Paul Cookson

Princess Poems

Clare Bevan

Could you be a princess?

A gorgeous collection of poems filled with tips on how to behave like a princess, meet the right prince and avoid the dangers posed by wicked stepmothers, dragons and unhappy fairy godmothers.

If You Were a Princess

If YOU were a princess, what would YOU ride?
A small, metal dragon
with cogwheels inside?
A horse with white feathers
and hooves of black glass?
A silvery unicorn
pounding the grass?
A fluttering carpet
that chases the bats?
A big, golden pumpkin
With coachmen like rats?
A castle that sways
on an elephant's back?
A long, steamy train
Going clickety clack?
Or a ship with blue sails
And YOUR name on the side?
If YOU were a princess, what would YOU ride?

A selected list of titles available from Macmillan Children's Books

The prices shown below are correct at the time of going to press. However, Macmillan Publishers reserves the right to show new retail prices on covers, which may differ from those previously advertised.

Space Poems

Gaby Morgan   ISBN-13: 978-0-330-44057-8   £3.99
                             ISBN-10: 0-330-44057-8

Fairy Poems

Clare Bevan   ISBN-13: 978-0-330-43352-5   £3.99
                             ISBN-10: 0-330-43352-0

Princess Poems

Clare Bevan   ISBN-13: 978-0-330-43389-1   £3.99
                             ISBN-10: 0-330-43389-X

Mermaid Poems

Clare Bevan   ISBN-13: 978-0-330-43785-1   £3.99
                             ISBN-10: 0-330-43785-2

All Pan Macmillan titles can be ordered from our website, www.panmacmillan.com, or from your local bookshop and are also available by post from:

Bookpost, PO Box 29, Douglas, Isle of Man IM99 1BQ
Credit cards accepted. For details:
Telephone: 01624 677237
Fax: 01624 670923
Email: bookshop@enterprise.net
www.bookpost.co.uk

Free postage and packing in the United Kingdom